HOW CAN I HELP
WHEN SOMEONE IS HURTING?

What can we do or say when someone we love –
family or friend – is facing long-term pain or illness?
We feel totally helpless. Can the fit and well have
anything to offer to those who are suffering?

The soft option is to walk away, leaving the person
totally alone. But there is another possibility.

In this challenging and thoughtful little book Philip
Yancey shares with us what he himself has learned
from people in pain. Although there may be little we
can say to help, there is plenty we can do. He gives
simple, practical advice that will help anyone in this
situation.

PHILIP YANCEY is the author of a number of
books, including the award-winning *Where Is God
When It Hurts?* (250,000 copies in print) and
Fearfully and Wonderfully Made. He is also a
freelance editor for *Christianity Today* and *Campus
Life* magazines. His home is in Chicago, USA.

Copyright © 1984 by Philip Yancey
Originally published in English
under the title *Helping the Hurting*
by Philip Yancey
Published by Multnomah Press
10209 SE Division, Portland, OR 972666 USA
All rights reserved

UK edition 1987
Published by
Lion Publishing plc
Icknield Way, Tring, Herts, England
ISBN 0 7459 1231 1
Albatross Books Pty Ltd
PO Box 320, Sutherland, NSW 2232, Australia
ISBN 0 86760 912 5

Photographs: Lion Publishing/David Townsend;
Mick Rock, Cephas Picture Library

Our thanks to the Bristol Cancer Help Centre
for their help with some of the photographs

British Library Cataloguing in Publication Data

Yancey, Philip
  How can I help when someone is hurting?
  1. Medicine——Religious aspects——
  Christianity
  I. Title
  248.8'6   BT732
  ISBN 0-7459-1231-1

Printed and bound in the Republic of Korea

HOW CAN I HELP WHEN SOMEONE IS HURTING?

PHILIP YANCEY

A LION BOOK
Tring · Batavia · Sydney

A few years ago I wrote a book called *Where Is God When It Hurts?*, and the letters that have come in response to that book have surprised me, moved me, and sometimes shamed me. Many have come from hospital rooms. Some were written by mothers of retarded children, and some by people with terminal illnesses who have since died.

I must confess that my contacts with suffering people have caused me more than a little embarrassment. In the first place, I enjoy fine health, interrupted only by a minor cold or sore throat every couple of years. I run twenty miles a week, in all weather, and do push-ups daily. Just about everything in my body works the way it is supposed to, and when I encounter suffering people I can't avoid a nagging sense of guilt.

But mainly I am embarrassed because I know myself too well. I give a seminar on 'The Problem of Pain', and afterwards a lady approaches me. She recounts a series of twenty-seven operations she has undergone to counteract the effects of a rare degenerative disease. She tells of would-be helpers who unwittingly compound her suffering, and describes to me her loneliness and self-hatred and despair—all the familiar emotions that seem to grow like a fungus inside hospital rooms. And then she says this: 'Your book is what saw me through. I don't know if I could have survived without it. You have such sensitivity and compassion. You must have endured great pain yourself.'

And I smile and thank her and talk some more, but inside I cringe because I know the truth. I know about my own good health and my relative unacquaintance with pain. And I also know that if I had visited that woman's hospital room, I would have offered her scant help.

I cannot imagine a less likely candidate for hospital visiting. I begin to clam up as soon as I go through the doors—because of the smell, I think. Smell has a direct sensory path into the brain, and those disinfectant odours trigger in me deep-seated memories of a childhood tonsillectomy. When a nurse in the corridor smiles and nods, I see a giant phantom nurse leaning over me with a plastic bag to smother me and steal my breath.

I have no file of comforting verses and prayers to deliver to patients. Whatever they say, I tend to agree with. When they voice their anger and despair, I too get angry and full of despair. I feel impotent to offer any genuine help to sick people. The problems seem just as baffling and maddening to me, standing alongside, as to the person who is suffering.

After several years of professional schizophrenia—writing and talking about pain while feeling personally helpless around it—I decided I should set aside my embarrassment and awkwardness and force myself to be near suffering people on a regular basis. About this time, a friend discovered he had one of the rarest, most severe forms of cancer. In medical history, the doctors told Jim, only twenty-seven people had been treated with his precise form of cancer. The other twenty-six had all died; Jim was alone.

He was thirty-three years old and had been

married only ten months. Earlier that year he and his wife had spent their honeymoon sailing in the Caribbean. Jim cared primarily about his career, his passion for downhill skiing, and his young marriage. Suddenly he faced the thought of dying, and he needed help.

At Jim's invitation I started accompanying him to a therapy group at a nearby hospital. People join therapy groups for a variety of reasons: to improve a self-image, to learn how to relate to others, to work through personal struggles. This therapy group consisted of people who were dying. They used the euphemism 'life-threatening illnesses' for their assortment of cancers, multiple sclerosis, severe hepatitis, muscular dystrophy, and other such diseases. But each member of the group knew that his or her life had boiled down to two issues: how to survive and, failing that, how to prepare for death.

The first meeting was very hard for me. We met in an open waiting-room area, sitting on cheap moulded plastic chairs of a garish orange colour that someone had probably chosen to make the institution appear more 'cheerful'. In the background, calls for doctors blared out over crackly loudspeakers and bored-looking porters wheeled trolleys up and down the corridors; inside our little cluster, thirty people tried to deal with issues of life and death.

The meeting began with each person 'checking in'. Someone had died in the month since the last meeting, and the social worker provided details of his last days and the funeral. Jim whispered to me that this was the one depressing part of the group: its members were always disappearing.

Most people were in their thirties. That age-group, normally so unaware of death, seemed to have the deepest need to talk about the great intruder. I had expected a tone of great sombreness at the meeting, but soon found the opposite. Tears flowed freely, of course, but these people talked easily and comfortably about disease and death. The group served as the one place in their lives where they *could* talk freely about how they really felt and count on an understanding response. Evidently I am not the only person who feels awkward in the presence of suffering people. They described sad and almost bizarre ways in which friends skirted the one thing that mattered most, the fact of their illness. But here in the group they let down all protective social barriers.

Nancy showed off a new wig, purchased to cover her baldness from chemotherapy treatment. She joked that she had always wanted straight hair and now her brain tumour had finally given her an excuse to get it. Steve, a young black man, admitted he was terrified of what lay ahead. He had battled with Hodgkin's disease as a teenager and had apparently won, but now, ten years later, symptoms had unexpectedly returned. Once again his body was trying to self-destruct.

I was most affected by the one elderly person in the room, a handsome, grey-haired woman with the broad, bony facial features of an Eastern European. She expressed her loneliness in simple sentences veiled in a thick accent. We asked if she had any family. An only son was trying to get emergency leave from the Air Force in Germany. And her husband? She swallowed hard a few times and then said, 'He came to see me just once. I was in the hospital. He brought me my bathrobe and a few things. The doctor stood in the

corridor and told him about my leukaemia.' Her voice started to crack and she dabbed at her eyes before continuing. 'He went home that night, packed up all his things, and left. I never saw him again.'

'How long had you been married?' I asked. Several people in the group gasped aloud at her answer: 'Thirty-seven years.' (I later learned that some researchers report a 70 per cent breakup rate in marriages in which one of the partners has a terminal illness; the tensions prove unbearable. In this group of thirty people, no marriages remained intact longer than two years—including my friend Jim's.)

I met with that group monthly for a year. Each person in it lived with the peculiar intensity that only death can bring. Certainly I cannot say that I 'enjoyed' the meetings—that would be the wrong word. Yet they became for me one of the most meaningful events of each month. In contrast to a party, where participants try to impress each other with signs of status and power and wit, at this group no one was trying to impress. Clothes, fashions, furniture, job titles, new cars—what do these things mean to people who are about to die?

I learned from them about pain. Among them I, who had the audacity to write a book on the subject, felt like the most ignorant of all people on earth. For a year I learned as a servant at the feet of teachers in the school of suffering.

I want to set down for you a few of the simple principles I gleaned.

I begin with some discouraging good news. The discouraging aspect is that I cannot give you a magic formula to deliver to suffering people. There is nothing much you can *say* to help. Some of the brightest minds in history have explored every angle of the problem of pain, asking why people hurt, and still we find ourselves stammering out the same questions. Not even God attempted an explanation of cause or rationale in his reply to Job. The great king David, the nearly perfect man Job, and finally even God in flesh, Jesus, reacted to pain much the same as we do. They recoiled from it, thought it horrible, did their best to alleviate it, and finally cried out to God in despair because of it. Personally, I find it discouraging that I have no final, satisfying answer for people in pain.

And yet, viewed in another way, that non-answer is surprisingly good news. When I have asked suffering people, 'Who helped you?' not one person has ever mentioned a PhD from theological college or a famous philosopher. The kingdom of suffering is a democracy, and we all stand in it or alongside it with nothing but our naked humanity. All of us have the same capacity to help, and that is good news.

The answer to the question 'How do I help those who hurt?' is exactly the same as the answer to the question 'How do I love?' A person in pain needs love, and not knowledge and wisdom. In this area of suffering, as in so many others, God uses very ordinary people to bring healing. And today, if you asked me for a Bible passage to teach you how to help suffering people, I would point to 1 Corinthians 13, the famous chapter on love.

Love breaks down into specific and practical ways to approach this particular group of people, those who hurt.

Making ourselves available

Instinctively, I shrink back from people who are in pain. Who can know whether they want to talk about their suffering or not? Do they want to be consoled or cheered up? What good can my presence possibly do? My mind spins out these rationalizations, and as a result I end up doing the worst thing possible: I avoid them.

Again and again, suffering people have told me the absolute necessity of people being available to them. It is not our words or our insights that they want most; it is our mere presence. 'Who helped you most?' I ask. They usually describe a quiet, unassuming person. Someone who was there whenever needed, who listened more than talked, who hugged and touched, and cried. Who didn't keep glancing down at a watch. Someone who was available, who came on the sufferer's terms and not their own. One woman in the group told us about her grandmother, a rather shy lady who had all the time in the world and simply sat in a chair and knitted while her granddaughter slept. She was available when any need arose.

We tend to disparage Job's three friends in the Bible for their insensitive response to his suffering. But what does the account say? When they came, they sat in silence beside Job for seven days and seven nights before opening their mouths. (As it turned out, those were the most eloquent moments they spent with him.)

Jewish people have a custom called *shiva* which they practise after a death in the community. For eight days friends, neighbours and relatives practically take over the house of the mourning person. They provide food, clean up, carry on conversation, and, in short, force their presence on the griever. The grieving person may wish for a time alone or a period of quietness, and may even find the presence of so many guests irritating. But the message comes through loudly: *We will not leave you alone. We will bear this pain with you.* In one highly symbolic meal, the visitors literally feed the mourner like a baby, placing food into his or her mouth with their own forks and spoons. The wisdom of the ages has taught their culture the need for a ritual, almost enforced availability. The mourner needs their presence whether or not he or she acknowledges the need.

What does one say at such a time? What messages of comfort can we offer? Consistently, I have received the same surprising answer from suffering people. It matters little what we say – our concern and availability matter far more. If we can offer a listening ear, that may be the most appreciated gift of all.

A story is told about Beethoven, a man not known for social grace. Because of his deafness, he found conversation difficult and humiliating. When he heard of the death of a friend's son, Beethoven hurried to the house, overcome with grief. He had no words of comfort to offer. But he saw a piano in the room. For the next half-hour he played the piano, pouring out his emotions in the most eloquent way he could. When he finished playing, he left. The friend later remarked that no one else's visit had meant so much.

Time restrictions put limits on our availability, of course, and not all of us have the freedom to offer large blocks of time. But we can all pray, a form of availability that may do more ultimate good than our personal presence. And we can

offer regular, consistent indications that we care. Suffering people say that regularity is often even more important than the quantity of time a person can give.

Betsy Burnham, in the book she wrote shortly before her death from cancer *(When Your Friend Is Dying)*, told of one of the most meaningful letters she received during her illness:

Dear Betsy,

I am afraid and embarrassed. With the problems you are facing, what right do I have to tell you I am afraid? I have found one excuse after another for not coming to see you. With all my heart, I want to reach out and help you and your family. I want to be available and useful. Most of all, I want to say the words that will make you well. But the fact remains that I am afraid. I have never before written anything like this. I hope you will understand and forgive me.

Love,
Anne

Anne could not find the personal strength needed to make herself available to her friend. But, unlike others, she took the time and care to share her honest feelings with Betsy and make herself vulnerable. That too was a form of availability.

The people in my hospital therapy group had long-term illnesses, the kind that will never go away. These call for a special kind of availability. People who struggle with long-term suffering report that a fatigue factor sets in. At first, no matter what the illness, they get a spurt of attention. Cards fill their letter-boxes, and flowers fight for space by their bedsides. But, as time goes by, attention fades.

We are embarrassed and troubled by problems that do not go away. In her book, Betsy Burnham reports that with each successive reappearance of her cancer, fewer visitors came to see her. As the illness stretched out, she felt even more vulnerable and afraid, and she also felt more alone. Some of her Christian friends seemed resentful that their prayers for healing had gone unanswered, almost as if they blamed her. They lost faith and stayed away. Betsy then had guilt and self-hatred to cope with in addition to her pain.

Parents of children with genetic defects echo Betsy's account. A flurry of sympathetic response follows the birth but soon fades. As the parents' needs and emotional difficulties increase, offers of help tend to decrease.

In the New Testament letters, Paul lists the 'fruit' which the Spirit of God produces in the lives of Christian people. He includes one that we translate with the ancient-sounding word 'longsuffering'. We would do well to revive that word, and concept, in its most literal form to apply to the problem of long-term pain.

Let me say this carefully, but say it nevertheless. I believe as a Christian that those who follow Christ are called to show love *when God seems not to*. People in pain, especially those with long-term pain, often have the sensation that God has left them. No one expressed this better than C. S. Lewis in the poignant journal he kept about his wife's death *(A Grief Observed)*. He recorded that at the moment of his most profound need,

God, who had seemed always available to him, suddenly seemed distant and absent, as if he had slammed a door shut and double-bolted it from the inside. That was how it felt.

Sometimes we must voice prayers that the suffering person cannot voice. And in moments of extreme pain or grief, very often God's love can only be perceived through ordinary people like you and me. In such a way we can, indeed, function as 'the body of Jesus Christ', to use a New Testament phrase.

Providing a sense of value

People in the hospital group referred to a process they called 'pre-mortem dying'. It occurs when well-intentioned relatives and friends look for ways to make the suffering person's last months trouble-free. 'Oh, you mustn't do that! I know you've always taken out the rubbish, but *really*, not in your condition. Let me do it.' And then, 'Don't burden yourself with balancing the cheque-book. It would just create an unnecessary worry for you. I'll take care of it from now on.'

Gradually, inexorably, everything that gives a person a sense of place or a role in life is taken away. A mother encourages her single daughter to sell her house and move back home. She does so, and discovers that in the process she has also lost her individual identity. Feelings of worth and value, already precarious because of the illness, slip further away.

Obviously, a very sick person needs to depend on others to cope with practical matters of life. But too easily we can fall into a pattern of removing everything that gives dignity.

Suffering people already question their place

in the world. Often they cannot continue working, and the fatigue brought on by illness or
treatment makes every action harder and more
tedious. Yet they, like all of us, need to cling to
something to remind them that they have a place,
that life would not go on without a bump if they
simply disappeared, that the cheque-book would
go unbalanced except for their expert attention.
Wise friends and relatives sense the delicate
balance between offering help and offering too
much help.

We live in a culture that has no natural 'place'
for sick people. We put them out of sight, behind
the walls of hospitals and nursing homes. We
make them lie in beds, with nothing to occupy
their time but the remote control devices that
operate the television sets. We even give them
the telling label 'invalid' (try pronouncing it a different way: in-*val*-id). And then, in a conscious
acknowledgment of their out-of-placeness, we
send them get-well cards.

I have made a study of get-well cards, and they
fall into distinct categories: schmaltzy ones with
pictures of flowers and corny poems, obscene
ones with messages about all the wild parties and
sex the recipient is missing, sincere ones with
a genuine conveyance of sympathy, clever ones
drawn by cartoonists. All have the same core
message, expressed in their title: 'get-well cards'.
One before me now has on the cover, 'Get well
soon . . .' and then inside, '. . . otherwise some-
body might steal your job.' Another: 'Everybody
hopes you feel better soon, except me . . .'
and inside, '. . . I hope you feel better right
now!' 'This is not time to be sick . . .' says
one of Boynton's hippos from a hospital bed,

'. . . the weekend's coming up.'

What complaint could I have with these innocuous messages? If you stand at a rack and study scores of similar cards, you begin to sense a subtle, underlying message: *There is something wrong with you. You don't fit, at work, at parties. You are missing out. You are invalid. You are not OK.*

Have you ever considered how a get-well card is read by people like those in my hospital therapy group, people who will never get well? For them, get-well cards do not uplift, and may produce despair. I sometimes threaten to produce my own line of cards. I already have an idea for the first one. The cover would read, in huge letters, perhaps with fireworks in the background, 'CONGRATULATIONS!!!' Then, inside, this message: '. . . to the 98 trillion cells in your body that are still working smoothly and efficiently.' I would look for ways to get across the message that a sick person is not a *sick person* but rather a person of worth and value who happens to have some bodily parts that are not functioning well. Perhaps the exercise of writing a series of cards like that would help me fight my own tendency to label whole persons as sick and eliminate a place for them in my society or church or family or school.

We who are friends and loved ones of sick people must look for ways to help them preserve a sense of place. For some, the answer will consist of very practical arts of service; for others, a structured way of helping other sick people through the same stages. Joni Eareckson, who became paralyzed as a result of a driving accident in her teens, beautifully recounts that the people who helped her most were the other paraplegics who devoted themselves to helping her through the roughest times. Now she completes the cycle by spending her own life helping others.

Some sick people have such reduced strength that they can do little but teach us about pain. Betsy Burnham channelled her own suffering into an endeavour that now teaches many others about helping the sick and dying. I found a very similar experience within the hospital therapy group, whose members taught me about pain— lessons I can now pass on to others. Everyone can find a sense of place, even if only recording the experience of suffering and helplessness.

Bringing meaning to the experience of suffering
Viktor Frankl, the famous psychologist, learned this definition while serving time in a Nazi concentration camp: 'Despair is suffering without meaning.' It follows, then, that those of us alongside suffering people should somehow find a way of bringing meaning or significance to their experiences.

Actually, we already convey meaning on a relative scale. We attribute different meanings to different kinds of suffering. When I give seminars on pain, I sometimes illustrate this by calling for audience participation. I ask for the Roman 'thumbs up' or 'thumbs down' signal when I mention an ailment: thumbs up if the pain is 'cool', acceptable, one which elicits immediate sympathy, and thumbs down if the pain is distasteful and gets little sympathy. Here are some of the comments and responses I get:

Broken leg from skiing. Thumbs up all the way. What started out as a fall on the rope tow ends up, after many retellings, as a double somersault free-fall off a cliff. Friends sign the cast with funny remarks, and the sufferer becomes a virtual hero.

Leprosy. Thumbs down. In fact, leprosy patients lobby strongly for the name 'Hansen's disease' for one simple reason: the way people respond to the image of leprosy. It is the least communicable of all communicable diseases and differs in almost every respect from its common image. Yet a person with leprosy usually gets judgment, not sympathy. Loneliness is one of the disease's worst aspects.

Influenza. Mixed response. Some people hold thumbs down because no one really *likes* fevers, vomiting, and body aches. On the other hand, because flu is so universal, it elicits much sympathy. We all know how it feels.

Mumps. Response depends on the age you're talking about. Children with mumps get plenty of sympathy. They are so fawned over that the illness, with all the ice cream you can eat, is almost worth the attention. But when an adult gets mumps, he is laughed at—even though mumps can have severe consequences for adults.

You could continue the list. *Haemorrhoids:* a very painful condition, but a social joke. *AIDS:* I know a few victims, and they hear a very clear message 'You deserve your pain'—and sometimes, from the church, 'God is punishing you.' I can hardly think of a more terrifying, devastating disease than AIDS, or one that provokes a less compassionate response.

Migraine headache, whiplash, cancer—each of these has a different 'image', and in subtle and sometimes blatant ways, we communicate a response to the sufferer that can make coping easier or harder.

At a different level, those of us who are Christians apply a further set of values to forms of suffering. We can judge pain, making its victims feel they have no meaning or perhaps a negative spiritual meaning. We can heap coals of fire on their suffering.

To a suffering person's pain we can add guilt: 'Haven't you prayed? Don't you have faith that God will heal you?' We can add self-doubt: 'Is there something God may be punishing you for? Have you confessed your anger and bitterness about this problem? Are you praising the Lord anyhow?' We can add confusion: 'What is God trying to tell you? Or is Satan causing this pain? Or simply natural providence? Or has God specially selected you as an example to others?'

I have interviewed enough suffering people to know that the pain caused by this kind of response can exceed the pain of the illness itself. Joyce Landorf poignantly describes the debilitation caused by TMJ (for temporomandibular joint dysfunction). The pain dominates her entire life. Yet, she says, it hurts far more when Christians write to her with judgmental comments based on their pet formulas of why God allows suffering.

If I were writing a full-length book, I would go through Romans 5, James 1, and 1 Peter 1 verse by verse for an inspired view of the meaning of suffering. Paul, Peter, and James do not focus on how to get suffering removed, or why it came in the first place, but rather on what good can possibly come from it.

Christian meaning with regard to suffering

comes from the pattern of redemption demonstrated on the cross. There, ultimate evil was transformed into ultimate good *despite* that terrible process of pain Jesus had to endure. We can rejoice, the apostles tell us, not because of our pain but because of what it produces. Each goes on to detail what suffering produces: patience (which can only be learned in circumstances that might easily produce impatience), perseverance, hope, etc. My own body, even when in revolt, self-destructing, collapsing against my will, can have meaning both for me and for those around me. We must strive to help people in pain find out what meaning their suffering can produce.

Henri Nouwen wrote an elegant little book with a wonderful title, *The Wounded Healer*, about some extreme examples. How can we offer meaning to people who have no meaning and no hope? He describes lonely, abandoned people who have no one to love them. What possible meaning can we bring to their pain? To such people our own loving concern may be the only meaning we can offer.

My wife works with some of the poorest people in our city: the elderly on welfare. She directs a church-sponsored programme that intentionally seeks out lonely and abandoned senior citizens. Many times I have seen her pour herself into someone's life, trying to convince the person that it *matters* whether he or she lives or dies. One woman, Mrs Kruider, had refused cataract surgery for twenty years. When she was seventy she had decided that nothing much was worth looking at and, anyhow, God must have wanted her blind if he made her that way.

It took Janet two years of cajoling, arguing,

persisting, and loving to convince Mrs Kruider to have cataract surgery. Finally she succeeded, for one reason: she impressed on her that it mattered to her, Janet, if Mrs Kruider had a chance to regain her sight. Mrs Kruider had given up on life; it held no meaning for her. But Janet transferred a meaning to her. It made a difference to someone that Mrs Kruider should not give up, even at ninety-two. At long last the old woman had the surgery.

In a literal sense, Janet shared Mrs Kruider's pain. That principle of shared pain is the thesis of Nouwen's book and perhaps the only sure contribution we can make to the problem of pain. In doing so, we follow God's pattern, for he too took on pain. He joined us and lived a life of more suffering and poverty than most of us will ever experience. Suffering can never ultimately be meaningless, because God himself has shared it. In a profound phrase, the letter to the Hebrews tells us that even Jesus 'learned through suffering'.

Offering hope

Alexander Solzhenitsyn, another concentration camp survivor, said these words: 'All that the downtrodden can do is go on hoping. After every disappointment they must find fresh reason for hope.' His words apply equally to people who suffer from long-term illness.

But what hope can we offer? There is the hope of eternal life and healing, of course, but can that make an actual, discernible difference to a person with a terminal disease?

In our increasing sophistication those of us who are Christians have, I think, grown a little ashamed of our faith's emphasis on immortality and rewards to come. I hear few sermons these days on this subject. Our culture screams at us that *suffering* is the reality—Ireland, Lebanon, El Salvador—and an afterlife promising immortality is just a pipe dream. Christians stand rightly accused by history of overlooking social ills because of a promise of 'pie in the sky by and by'.

But is there any other sure hope to offer? And is the hope of an afterlife and eternal healing a worthy hope? To answer that question, I must tell you the story of Martha, one of the members of the hospital therapy group. In a sense, her story summarizes everything I learned about pain in my year with the group.

Martha caught my eye at the very first meeting. Other people there had obvious signs of illness: thinning hair, a sallow complexion, a missing limb, an uncontrolled trembling. But Martha showed no such symptoms. She was twenty-six and very attractive. I wondered if she, like me, had come with a friend.

When it came to Martha's turn to speak, she said she had just contracted ALS, or Lou Gehrig's disease. Her father had died of the same disease a year before, and two years before that her uncle had died of it. ALS rarely shows hereditary connections and very rarely attacks young women, but somehow she had cruelly defied the odds.

ALS destroys nerve control. It first attacks voluntary movements, such as control over arms and legs, then hands and feet. It progresses on to involuntary movements, finally affecting breathing and causing death. Sometimes a person's body succumbs quickly, sometimes not. Martha's relatives had lived through two years of degeneration before death. Martha knew the pattern in excruciating detail.

My first meeting with the group took place in March. In April, Martha arrived in a wheelchair. She could walk only with great difficulty and because of that had just been fired from her job at a university library.

By May Martha had lost the use of her right arm and could no longer use crutches. She operated the manual wheelchair with great difficulty. By June she had lost the use of both arms and could barely move the hand controls on a new electric wheelchair.

I began visiting Martha at her rehabilitation hospital. I took her for short rides in her wheelchair and sometimes picked her up for the group meetings. I learned about the indignity of her suffering. I learned to check her toes before putting on her shoes—if they were curled, they would jam painfully in the shoe. I learned to close her hand and guide it carefully into her jacket—otherwise her fingers would catch in the sleeve. I also had to watch for her dangling arms before setting her down on the car seat. It is not easy to position a nine-stone body of dead weight inside a small car.

Martha needed help with every move: getting dressed, arranging her head on the pillow, cleaning her bedpan. When she cried, someone else had to wipe her tears and hold a tissue to her nose. Her body was in utter revolt against her will. It would not obey any of her commands.

We talked about death and, briefly, about Christian hope. I confess to you readily that the great Christian hopes of eternal life, ultimate healing, and resurrection sounded thin as smoke when held up to someone like Martha. She wanted not angel wings but an arm that would not flop to the side, a mouth that did not drool, and lungs that would not collapse on her.

She thought about God, of course, but she could hardly think of him with love. She held out against any deathbed conversion, insisting that, as she put it, she would only turn to God out of love and not out of fear. And how could she love a God who did this to her?

It became clear around October that ALS would complete its horrible cycle quickly. Martha soon had to practise breathing with a toy-like plastic machine. She blew as hard as she could to make little blue balls rise in the pressure columns. Between gasps for breath, she talked about which she preferred losing first, her voice or her breath. Ultimately she decided she would rather her lungs went first; she preferred dying to dying mute, unable to express herself. Because of reduced oxygen supply to her brain, she tended to fall asleep in the middle of conversations. Sometimes at night she would wake up in a panic, with a sensation like choking, and be unable to call for help.

Despite logistical problems, Martha managed to make one last trip to a favourite summer cabin in the country and to her mother's home nearby. She was making final preparations, saying her last farewells. She badly wanted at least two weeks in her own flat, as a time to invite her friends over, one by one, in order to say goodbye and to come to terms with her death.

But the two weeks in her flat posed a problem. How could she stay there? Government aid would keep her in a hospital room, but not at home, not with the intensive service she needed just to stay alive.

Only one group in the whole city offered the

free and loving personal care that Martha needed. A Christian community adopted Martha as a project and volunteered to fulfil her last wishes. Sixteen women rearranged their lives for her. They divided into work teams, traded off baby-sitting duties for their own children, and moved in. They stayed with Martha, listened to her ravings and complaints, bathed her, helped her sit up, moved her, watched her all night, prayed for her, and loved her. They were available. They gave her a place and gave meaning to her suffering. To Martha, they were the living embodiment of God.

These women also explained to Martha the Christian hope. And finally Martha, having seen the love of God enfleshed—when God himself seemed uncompassionate, even cruel—came to that God in Christ and presented herself in trust to the one who had died for her. She did not come to God in fear; she found his love at last. In a moving service, she feebly testified to her faith and was baptized.

On the day before Thanksgiving in 1983, Martha died. Her body, crumpled, misshapen, atrophied, was a pathetic imitation of its former beauty. When it finally stopped functioning, Martha left it.

But today Martha lives, in a new body, in wholeness and triumph. She lives because of the victory that Christ won and because of his body, the church, who made that victory known to her. And if I or any of Christ's followers does not believe that, and if our Christian hope, tempered by sophistication, does not allow us to offer that truth to a dying, convulsing world, then we are indeed, as Paul said, 'of all men most miserable'.